The Right Bite

Contents

Written by Rachel Delahaye

Collins

Shark bite

The Great White shark is one of the most efficient eaters in the animal kingdom. They have around 300 **serrated** teeth, arranged in about seven rows.

Just right ...

for tearing and chomping fish and mammals.

Just right ...
for crunching fish
and shrimps.

4

Crocodile teeth

Crocodile teeth are **conical** and of varying sizes.

Extra bite

Crocodiles have strong, forceful teeth, but they cannot chew! They swallow their prey whole.

Just right ... for wounding and trapping.

Crocodile teeth close like a cage of knives.

5

Small nibblers

If you have holes in your house, they are usually caused by rodents.

These small animals have huge incisors that slice like a pair of scissors. Their back teeth, called molars, help with chewing.

incisors

Just right ... for cutting food and wood.

Rabbits have an extra set of incisors. With these "peg teeth" they are able to grip food tightly without using their paws!

Rodents' and rabbits' teeth never stop growing. They have to wear their teeth down by grinding them and gnawing hard substances.

Extra bite

"Rodent" comes from a Latin word that means *to **gnaw***.

Do snails have teeth?

Snails have a *radula*, lined with tiny spikes called *denticles*. There are up to 25,000 of them!

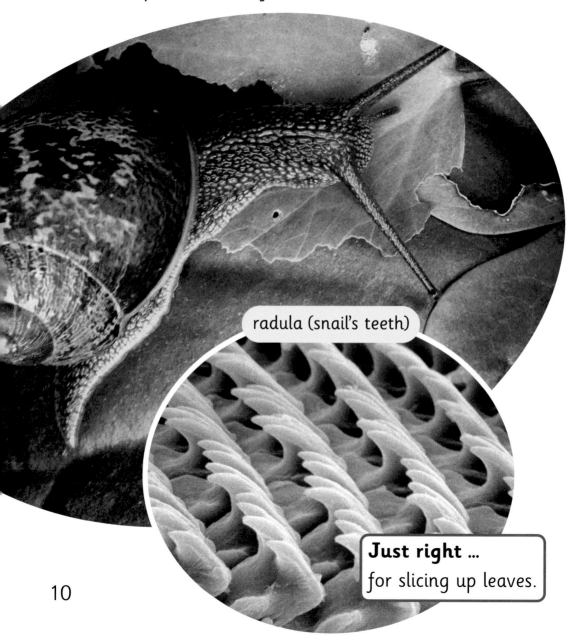

radula (snail's teeth)

Just right ...
for slicing up leaves.

Crabeater seal

These teeth mesh so that water drains out, leaving food trapped inside the mouth.

Just right ...
for catching krill.

Extra bite
Crabeater seals don't eat crabs!

11

Meat eaters

Animals that eat meat have three kinds of teeth.

Extra bite

A pet cat has the same kinds of teeth as a lion.

small incisors — to grip and tear

big canines — to stab and rip

even bigger teeth –
for crunching bones

Just right ...
for catching, wounding
and tearing.

13

Green grazers

Some animals have a diet of plants.

> **Just right …**
> for breaking down grass and leaves.

> **Extra bite**
> Grazers' jaws move sideways to help with the grinding process.

14

little incisors at the front for ripping

large flat molars at the back for grinding

15

Meat and vegetables

Some animals, like humans, eat **vegetation** *and* meat.

incisors for gripping
and snipping

canines for tearing
and ripping

molars for crunching
and crushing

17

Toothless wonders

Some animals have no teeth.

Tortoises have beaks
to slice vegetation.

spines

Anteaters have sticky spines to grab ants.

Many insects have mandibles to cut, crush and fight.

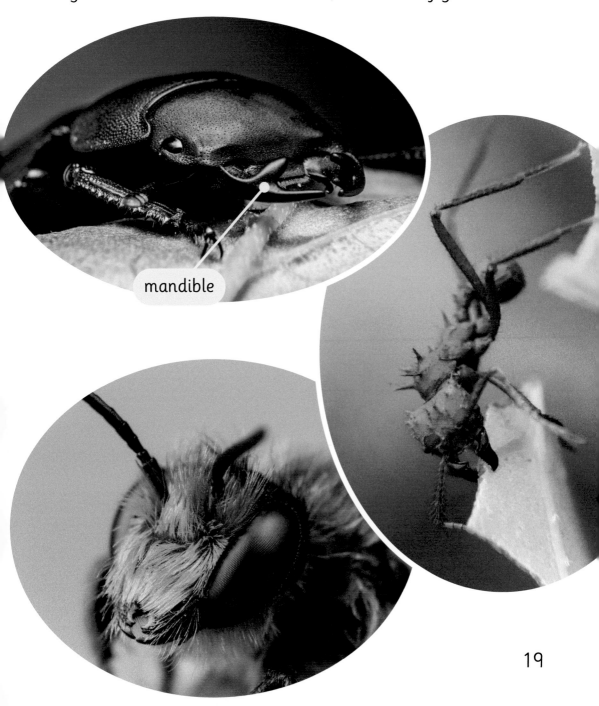

mandible

Each animal has the right bite for the food it needs!

Glossary

Conical cone-shaped
Gnaw chew
Serrated with a jagged edge
Vegetation plants

21

The right bite

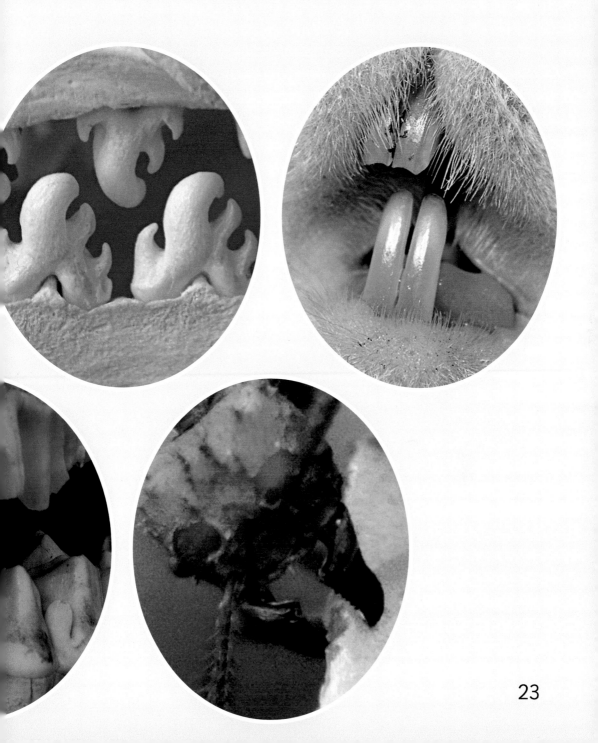

After reading

Letters and Sounds: Phases 5–6

Word count: 455

Focus phonemes: /n/ kn, gn /s/ c, ce, sc /sh/ ti, ci /zh/ s

Common exception words: of, to, the, are, do, their, one, whole, water

Curriculum links: Science: Animals, including humans

National Curriculum learning objectives: Reading/word reading: apply phonic knowledge and skills as the route to decode words; read accurately by blending sounds in unfamiliar words containing GPCs that have been taught; read common exception words, noting unusual correspondences between spelling and sound and where these occur in the word; read other words of more than one syllable that contain taught GPCs; Reading/comprehension: develop pleasure in reading, motivation to read, vocabulary and understanding by being encouraged to link what they read or hear to their own experiences

Developing fluency

- Your child may enjoy hearing you read the book.
- Take turns to read a page of the main text, pausing at commas, ellipses (...) and between sentences.

Phonic practice

- Focus on words with more than one syllable and /n/ and /s/ sounds.
- Challenge your child to read the following, breaking the words into syllables if necessary to help them.
  in-cis-ors   sub-stan-ces   gnaw-ing   sciss-ors   gnash-ers
- On pages 2 and 3, can they find another word that starts with two letters that have the /n/ sound? (*knife*)

Extending vocabulary

- Look at the Glossary on page 21. Discuss other words that could be in this glossary, e.g. incisors, molars, canines. Challenge your child to decide on a definition for each word.

Comprehension

- Turn to pages 22 and 23. Discuss the way in which each set of teeth suits the creature and what it eats.
- Ask your child:
  o On page 11, how do crabeater seals catch krill? (e.g. *they grab a mouthful of water – the krill are trapped in their mouths but the water drains out*)